O9-AIC-707

REAL HAPPINESS
The Workbook

Creating Your Personal Roadmap
to a Joyful and Empowered Life

Paul Ferrini

Book Design by Paul Ferrini
and Lisa Carta

ISBN # 978-1-879159-71-6

Copyright 2007 by Paul Ferrini
All rights reserved including the right of
reproduction in whole or in part or in any form.

Heartways Press
9 Phillips Street, Greenfield MA 01301
www.heartwayspress.com

Manufactured in the United States of America

Table of Contents

Introduction

Real Happiness and Emotional Healing

All of us can learn to be more genuinely happy than we are. But in order to do so, we have to be willing to take our masks off and face our pain head on. We have to see where we hurt and begin to heal our childhood wounds. Until the child within us has healed his or her trauma, the adult cannot truly be happy. Emotional healing and Real Happiness go hand in hand.

This Workbook is best used in conjunction with the companion book entitled *Real Happiness, A Roadmap for Healing our Pain and Awakening the Joy that is Our Birthright.* You will also find two other books — *The Hidden Jewel* and *Embracing Our True Self* — to be very helpful in understanding the roadmap to healing and empowerment presented in this book.

If you bought this book at a *Real Happiness Workshop* you have already taken a major step forward in transforming your life. If you purchased this book in a bookstore, feel free to begin doing the exercises and spiritual practices in this book on your own. If you need help or just want to go deeper into the material, please call us at 1-888-427-8929 to find out when and where the next *Real Happiness Workshop* will be offered. Working with others in a group setting is a very powerful way to do this work and I strongly recommend it.

Definition of Real Happiness

When we talk about real happiness, we are not talking about "pretend" or "phony" happiness. We are not talking about the Madison Ave. or overly idealized kind of happiness we see on billboards or television commercials. That doesn't exist for anyone. That is a myth.

By real happiness we mean the ability to be true to ourselves, kind to others, and able to weather the ups and downs of life with acceptance and compassion.

There are two primary areas where happiness is found: relationship with self, and relationship with others.

A genuinely happy person knows or is learning to:

1. Accept, nurture and love him or herself.
2. Live honestly and authentically.
3. Make his or her own decisions and accept responsibility for them.
4. Develop his or her talents and gifts and find his or her passion and purpose.
5. Cultivate an open heart and an open mind.

A genuinely happy person knows or is learning to:

1. Love and accept others.
2. Honor their uniqueness and encourage them to be true to themselves.
3. Empower them to make their own decisions and to take responsibility for them.
4. Support them in developing their talents and standing in their power and purpose.
5. Encourage them to be open in heart and mind.

This is done not by preaching, but by modeling these capacities. A genuinely happy person has the following attributes:

- Compassion for self and others
- The ability to forgive and learn from his/her mistakes and those of others
- Patience with the process of healing and transformation
- A positive attitude toward life and the ability to see obstacles as challenges
- A belief in the essential goodness of all beings and their worthiness of love

A genuinely happy person lives in *Right Relationship* to self and others and engages in *Right Livelihood*, expressing his or her gifts and bringing joy to self and others. These are therefore the goals of this work.

What we are Healing/Transforming

In order to bring something new in, we must be prepared to let something go that we no longer need. There are many ways that we betray ourselves and others that we must learn to relinquish if we want to heal and step into our power. Here are a few of the changes that will occur when we commit to our process of emotional healing.

We learn to relinquish:	*We replace it with:*
Self Judgment/Condemnation	Self Acceptance/Love
Shame/Unworthiness	Innocence/Self Worth
Being Invisible or Silent	Allowing Ourselves to be Seen and Heard
Isolation/Emotional Disconnection	Community/Emotional Connection
Giving Our Power Away	Stepping into our Power and Purpose
Blaming Others	Taking Responsibility
Judging Others	Looking at our Triggers and our Wound
Stuffing or Running from Our Fear	Being with our Fear Compassionately
Pleasing Others	Honoring Ourselves
Controlling Others	Giving Others Permission to be Themselves
Being Abused or Engulfed	Saying No and Setting Limits
Working for Others	Working with Others
Ignoring or Disparaging our Gifts	Trusting and Expressing our Gifts
Running Away from Love	Acknowledging our Fear of Intimacy
Attacking Others	Owning Our Anger and not Projecting it
Blaming/Attacking Ourselves	Forgiving/Being Gentle with Ourselves
Perfectionism	Realistic Expectations of Self/Others
Addictive Patterns	Facing the Pain Behind them
Lack of Confidence/Failure	Taking Small Steps/Taking Pressure Off
Negativity	Cultivating a Positive Attitude

The Steps in the Healing Process

1. We remove our masks and share honestly with others.

We own our fear, our shame, our pain and dysfunction using the Affinity Process in dyads and small groups (see my book *Living in the Heart*). The process creates a safe space of unconditional love and acceptance and helps us open our hearts, acknowledge our pain, and walk through our fears. You can experience the *Affinity Process* by joining one of our free telephone affinity groups (see the website www.paulferrini.com).

2. We identify our present pain/distress and trace it back to our core wound.

Many of us have pain in our work and relationships, or we have addictions or health issues that are challenging us. Behind our present pain are wounds and traumas that go back to childhood or even in utero. Many of the exercises in this book can help us to touch the places in our hearts that hurt most.

3. We understand the nature of our self-betrayal and why it must come to an end.

As we get in touch with our wound and the reactive behavior patterns that arise from it, we see how we have given our power away to please others and win their love and approval. We have created a False Self that prevents us from being who we are authentically. We come to understand why the False Self must die for the True Self to be born.

4. We stop betraying ourselves and step into our power and purpose.

When we decide to be true to ourselves, our lives change. We overcome self limiting patterns, walk through our fears and learn to trust our wings. Our relationships are challenged to become more honest and authentic. We can no longer do work that does not give us joy or offer us an opportunity to express our talents and gifts. We emerge from the cocoon of the healing process not as the caterpillar who entered it but as the butterfly with brightly colored wings. Our inner beauty moves to the surface. We become who we always were but were afraid to be. We become real.

5. Once we become real, real happiness is possible for us.

We just need to continue the process of healing that we have begun here. Our *Real Happiness Workshop* will help you go deeper into the process of self-transformation. It will also introduce you to our healing community where you will meet others who are healing their wounds, overcoming self betrayal and stepping into their power and purpose in life.

I hope that you find this workbook helpful in understanding and healing your core wound and opening your heart to love without conditions. I would love to hear about your experiences doing this work.

Namaste,

Paul Ferrini

Real happiness means embracing our True Self,
nurturing our gift and giving it to the world.

PART 1

Real and Unreal Happiness

Happiness is an Internal State

There are two types of happiness: real happiness and unreal happiness. Real happiness comes from within. It is unconditional. No one can take it away from you. Unreal happiness comes from the outside. That means that it is conditional and can easily be threatened or taken away from you.

You can have a perfect life on the outside and be miserable on the inside. You can have a great job, lots of money, a wonderful family, a boat, a plane, a luxury car, and still go out one day and jump off a bridge.

Money or material possessions cannot make you happy. A relationship or a job cannot make you happy. Social status or public recognition cannot make you happy. No external condition can make you happy. Conversely, no external condition makes you unhappy. You may think that lack of money, or work or relationship is making you unhappy, but that is an erroneous belief.

Real happiness comes from connection with your Core Self. It leads naturally to right relationship, right livelihood, and all the other components of self-fulfillment. In the same manner, unhappiness arises from lack of connection with your Core Self.

Many of us believe that our happiness is based on what we "have" or on what we "do." But real happiness is not based on anything that we have or anything that we do. Real happiness is based on "who" we are and "how" we are. It is based on our relationship with our Core Self. That is because happiness is an internal state, not an external condition.

Please use the journal space below to reflect on the idea that genuine happiness cannot come from the outside, but only from within. What does this mean for you?

∞ Journal Notes ∞

Myths about Happiness

Our fairy tales tell us that it is possible to live "happily ever after," but that is a myth.

Real happiness is a journey we take with many ups and downs, peaks and valleys. As a result, we are not always happy on the journey of happiness. Sometimes we are sad. Sometimes we hurt. Sometimes we are angry.

We are learning to be more happy, more accepting, and more forgiving. We are learning to experience the highs of life without getting ego inflated and to experience the lows without being devastated. We are learning to hold all of our experience with love and compassion.

A happy person knows how to be sad and still love himself. He knows how to accept his experience as it is and to learn whatever lessons it brings.

In the space below, describe your idea and experience of happiness. What happiness myths do you have?

๑ Journal Notes ๑

Pretending to be Happy

We all pretend to be happy when we are not. We all pretend that it doesn't hurt when it does hurt. There are many ways in which we live in pretense or denial, wearing a mask to hide our pain. When we wear a happy mask or make a smiley face over our pain, our happiness is fake and our pain is merely stuffed or disguised.

To discover real happiness, we must learn to take the mask off and face our pain directly. To be happy we can't be in denial of our pain. We have to learn to love ourselves through it.

Use the space below to consider whether or not you are hiding your pain and pretending to be happy. Do you know what your mask is? Are you willing to take it off and face the pain behind it?

❀ Journal Notes ❀

Getting in Touch with Your Pain

If you have difficulty getting in touch with your pain, begin to look at the relationships that push your buttons. Who and what triggers you? What do you do when you are triggered? Do you stuff your pain? Do you attack others? Do you shut down emotionally and become inaccessible? Use the space below to describe who and what triggers you and what you do with your pain.

∞ Journal Notes ∞

Finding the Root of the Pain

If you look deeply, you will see that your present pain is rooted in the past. Usually it goes back to your childhood. If you want to heal your pain, you have to have to find the root—the core wound—understand it and forgive it.

You will be doing more work with this later, but for now just take a few moments to trace your pain back and make a note of the most painful moments in your life. When, where and with whom did you feel the most hurt? Write down everything you remember. Then look at it and see if you can see a pattern or a theme. Can you connect the dots?

∞ Journal Notes ∞

Taking Responsibility for Healing Your Pain

We all experience judgment, criticism and attack from others. We may also experience abandonment or betrayal. We need to see all this without investing our energy in blaming others. The goal of this work is not to justify our anger toward others, to judge them or to punish them. The goal of this work is to heal from our wounds.

In order to heal, we need to understand that others hurt us because they themselves have been hurt. They are merely passing onto us what was done to them. This does not excuse them for what they did. They will still need to atone for their actions. But that is their journey, not ours.

To heal, you must move through your shame and forgive yourself for what happened. You must realize that you did not deserve to be hurt. You were not and are not bad or unworthy. You may feel that you are, but that is your shame. To heal you must remove the cloak of shame your wound is wrapped in. You must feel the pain, move through it, and recover your innocence.

Please use the space below to describe how much of this work you have done and how much you still need to do. How much are you blaming others for what happened as opposed to taking responsibility for healing your wound?

๑๑ Journal Notes ๑๑

Medicating the Pain

Sometimes we have a hard time accessing our pain because we have learned to medicate it. Addiction becomes a way in which we try to live with our wound without healing it.

To avoid feeling our pain, we may abuse drugs or alcohol. We may try to fill the hole in our hearts with food, sex or work. This behavior may dull down our pain or divert our attention away from it, but it doesn't make the pain go away.

The more we ignore our pain or try to make it go away, the more it intensifies. Like magma seething in the depths of a volcano, our pain gets increasingly volatile. The pressure builds up until our pain erupts.

When doses or quantities of the substance we abuse spiral out of control, our addiction becomes part of our pain, instead of the band-aid over it. That is when the game is up and our pain bleeds through the mask. We are out of control and others see it.

If you have tried to medicate your pain so that you don't have to feel it, please use the space below to describe your specific addiction and the help you have sought to deal with it.

While addictions can and must be treated, they are the symptom of the dis-ease, not the cause of it. Do you know what the cause of your pain is and why you are afraid to face it?

∞ Journal Notes ∞

The Litmus Test for Real Happiness

Below are 30 Questions. Your answers to these questions will reveal just how happy you really are. Put a 5 next to the question if you can wholeheartedly answer "yes" to it. Put a 1 next to it if you can clearly answer "no" without reservations. Enter a 4 if it is a "weak yes" (more a yes than a no) and a 2 if it is "weak no" (more no than yes.). Put a 3 next to it if you cannot say yes or no. Please answer these questions honestly if you want accurate results.

____ 1. Do you accept yourself deeply, profoundly and without conditions?

____ 2. Do you understand that you are innocent and worthy of love and practice bringing love and compassion to yourself on a daily basis?

____ 3. Do you understand that others are also innocent and worthy of love and practice bringing love and compassion to others every day?

____ 4. Have you forgiven yourself for your mistakes/trespasses—big ones and small ones—and have you learned from these errors so that you won't repeat them?

____ 5. Have you forgiven others for their trespasses against you—big ones and small ones—and have you learned from these experiences so that you won't attract similar situations in the future?

____ 6. Are you in touch with your anger and able to express it without condemning or attacking others?

____ 7. Are you criticizing yourself progressively less and learning increasingly to hold your judgments of self with compassion?

____ 8. Are you criticizing others progressively less and learning increasingly to hold your judgments of others with compassion?

____ 9. Do you stand up for yourself in a loving way and set limits with others who try to take advantage of you or control you?

____ 10. Do you consistently take responsibility for your own thoughts, feelings and actions and communicate with others in an honest, non-blaming way?

____ 11. Are you in touch with your gifts and talents and are you actively expressing them?

____ 12. Do you have meaningful work that is in harmony with your life purpose?

____ 13. Are you financially solvent? Do you live within your means? Are you at peace with the amount of money/possessions that you have?

____ 14. Do you express yourself creatively? Do you have an activity/hobby that you do regularly for the sheer joy of it? Do you take time to play and have fun?

____ 15. Do you take time to smell the roses and appreciate the small things in life? Do you savor the beauty that unfolds in and around your life?

____ 16. Do you spend some time alone and connect with your core self on a regular basis?

____ 17. Are you in a stable relationship in which intimacy and trust continue to grow? If you are not in a relationship, please answer this question and the next two based on your last relationship.

____ 18. Do you consistently spend quality time with your partner and communicate honestly?

____ 19. When your partner triggers you, can you take responsibility for your feelings and tell your partner how hurt or angry you feel without blaming him/her? Can you work through your triggers and come to peace with each other?

____ 20. Are you able to accept your children and guide them lovingly without needing to criticize them or control them? If you do not have children, please put a 3 here.

____ 21. Are you at peace with your parents? Do you understand their pain and trauma and have you forgiven them for the ways in which they may have hurt you?

____ 22. Are you doing something in your life to serve or care for others without asking for anything in return?

____ 23. Are you taking good care of your body with a proper diet, daily exercise and enough restful sleep?

____ 24. Are you free of addictions or dependencies on recreational or prescription drugs, alcohol or other substances that impair or reduce your mental alertness?

____ 25. Are you primarily free of worries/anxieties/paranoia? Have you found an effective way of resolving or discharging physical, mental or emotional tension when you are feeling stressed out?

____ 26. Have you found a way to work with your fears and negative thoughts so that they do not run your life and prevent you from seeing the opportunities for good that surround you?

____ 27. Do you believe in the basic goodness of human beings and know that the vast majority of people do not deliberately try to hurt others?

____ 28. Do you feel connected to a higher power or spiritual source that you can turn to for love, acceptance, guidance, and support when you need it?

____ 29. Do you have friends you can trust who accept you the way you are and encourage you to be true to yourself?

____ 30. Do you have family members you can trust who accept you the way you are and encourage you to be true to yourself?

____ 31. Are you a member of a supportive spiritual family, group or community that accepts and loves you unconditionally?

____ 32. Are you feeling reasonably fulfilled in your life? If this were your last day on the planet, would you feel that your life has been meaningful and that you have made a positive contribution to the world in which you live?

____ 33. Do you feel that you have learned the lessons of your embodiment and are accomplishing the work you came here to do?

_____ Total Score

Interpreting the Results

Now add up all of the numbers. The highest score you can get is 165. Anyone who has a score from 132-165 is really happy. Anyone with a score from 99–132 is moderately happy. Anyone with a score from 66-99 is moderately unhappy. Anyone with a score of 33-66 is really unhappy.

The goal of this exercise is not to get a high score, but to get an accurate score. That means you don't want to be too generous or too hard on yourself when you answer these questions. Yet, regardless of how objective you are, the results of this *Litmus Test for Real Happiness* are subjective. They reflect how you see yourself. If you are in denial of your pain, you could get an unrealistically high score. It you are identified with the pain in your life, you could get an unrealistically low score. Only you can decide how accurate your score is and what you can learn from it.

Toward that end, please take a look at those questions that you answered with a 1 or a 2. Those are the areas of your life where improvement is possible. Improvement may involve learning new skills, developing a more positive attitude, or both. Take some time now to journal about how and where improvement is possible for you.

PART 2

Showing up for Your Life

Three Requirements for Real Happiness

To be happy you need to be willing to show up for your life. You cannot run away from yourself or from others. You can't crawl into a cave and disappear. You can't think that other people control your happiness. They don't.

There is only one person who controls your happiness or lack of it and that is you.

To be happy, you need to show up for life and take responsibility for what you think, feel, say and do. You can't blame anyone else for your woes. Blame and shame keep you locked into unhappiness. They are a big part of the story that needs to go.

Here are three things you need to do to be happy:

1) Show up for your life. (Stop running away.)

2) Take responsibility for your thoughts, feelings, and actions. (Stop blaming others.)

3) Stop believing that others can make you happy. (They can't.)

Please use the space below to indicate the ways in which you have run away, blamed others, or looked for happiness through others. Are you willing start showing up, taking responsibility and cultivating happiness from the inside out?

๏ Journal Notes ๏

Commit to the Journey

Cultivating happiness from the inside out will require some reprogramming. Your mind/body circuits will need to be rewired. Synapses must learn to fire differently.

All this requires time, patience, and commitment to the journey of healing. It requires taking small steps and celebrating small victories. It is a gradual process. It cannot be speeded up. You cannot skip steps. Like the turtle you must move forward at a slow, steady pace. That insures that you will stay grounded and focused and that you will be able to integrate the new energies that come into your life.

Use the journal space below to consider how patient and committed you are to a process of transformation that does not produce results overnight. Can you show up day by day? Can you be satisfied taking the small steps and doing the daily practices that will eventually lead to insights and breakthroughs? Or do you insist on having results right away?

∞ Journal Notes ∞

Invest in Yourself and Your Life

Are you willing to make an investment in your life? Are you willing to do your emotional healing and begin to develop the gifts and talents that you have? Are you in for the long haul or are you looking for a quick fix?

I recently met with the regional director for a large hotel chain. He had been in the business for 35 years. His first job was washing dishes. Then he became a front desk clerk. Gradually he worked his way up to General Manager. He talked about his career with a twinkle in his eyes. He was proud of what he had achieved and well he should be.

However, I must tell you, I know many people who are "too proud" to take a job as a dishwasher. They want to be General Manager first. They want to skip the steps.

People who try to skip steps usually fall flat on their faces. They fail time and time again. They haven't learned to show up each day and do the little things that are necessary to succeed.

When I ask if you are willing to make an investment in your life, I am talking about what you are willing to do today and tomorrow and every day for the next month. I am not talking about what you are going to do twenty years from now.

Use the space below to describe the investment you are willing to make in yourself. What talents/gifts do you need to develop? What skills do you need to learn? What concrete steps are you willing to take right now to heal and empower yourself?

❧ Journal Notes ❧

Let Go of Victim Consciousness

Some of us have a hard time moving forward in our lives because we are fearful and haunted by past failures. We get stuck in negative thinking and focus on what we can't do or what won't work. As a result, we keep creating the past over and over again.

We are good victims and complainers. We say, "I can't hit the ball" when we haven't even shown up to the batting cage to take our practice swings. Our negative expectations and lack of willingness to take the steps that are necessary to improve our lives creates a kind of paralyzing inertia and powerlessness. By dwelling on our fear and perceived limitations, we recreate the conditions of our suffering over and over again.

If this sounds like you, it is time to make a real change in the way you think and talk to yourself. So, starting now, stop telling yourself or others what you *can't do* and why you can't do it. That's just your story. And it does not empower you. It keeps you stuck in your victimhood. Instead, say what you *can do*. That is where you must begin.

Use the space below to make a list of what you can do to improve your life. What are the little steps you can take to develop more of a positive mind set and take advantage of the opportunities in front of you?

∞ Journal Notes ∞

Cultivate a Positive Attitude

Saying "Yes" when you mean it is the most powerful way to embrace life. When everyone says "Yes," mountains are moved and miracles happen. I have seen this occur time and time again.

However, people often put obstacles in the way of any venture. They get ego-involved, critical, and find hundreds if not thousands of reasons why they can't say, "Yes." By so doing, they discount opportunities that could bring new energy into their lives.

That's why it is important to cultivate a positive attitude. This does not mean pretending to be happy or stuffing your pain. It simply means seeing the opportunities for good that surround you. Every day, we are surrounded with opportunities to grow, to learn and to move forward in our lives. The universe has many gifts to offer us if we are open to receive them. Our job is to stay open and not to shut down our hearts or close our eyes.

You can experiment with the power of positive thinking by taking one day of your life and saying "Yes" to every opportunity for growth that presents itself. Keep your heart and your mind open throughout the day. When the door opens, walk through it. See what happens and then come back here and journal it.

๑๑ Journal Notes ๑๑

Recognize Negativity

Many of us have developed a habitual way of looking at life with a negative bias and, as a result, we do not see things clearly or accurately. If you don't believe me, try this experiment. For one day, make a list of every time you say, "Yes, I can" or "No, I can't." In the left box below, write down the positive, hopeful things that you think or say. In the right box, write down your negative, critical words or thoughts.

Anytime you express joy or gratitude, write it on the left side. Anytime you criticize or complain, write it on the right side.

Please be honest; don't cheat one way or the other. At the end of the day, see which box has the most entries. That will give you some idea of just how negative or positive your attitude is.

The goal of this exercise is not to encourage you to see life through rose-colored glasses. You are not being asked to see only the bright side of life and ignore the dark side. That would be taking the practice to the other extreme. The goal here is to see life in a more balanced way so that you can appreciate the gifts and show up for the challenges that come your way.

∾ Positive, Hopeful Words or Thoughts ∾	∾ Negative, Critical Words or Thoughts ∾

PART 3

Meeting the Core Self, The False Self and the True Self

Radical Self Acceptance

Most of us have no idea what radical self-acceptance means. That is probably because we have no idea of who we really are. We know our False Self, but we do not know our True Self. To meet the True Self, we need to let go of everything that is false or untrue about us. We have to drop our masks. We have to shed our old skin.

The True Self is not a victim and can never be. To meet the True Self, we need to drop our story of who we think we are and let go of all the reasons why we believe that we can't be happy. None of these stories is true and they just keep our unhappiness in place.

Please use the space below to describe some of the masks and stories that you need to relinquish in order to encounter your True Self.

✿✿ Journal Notes ✿✿

Connecting with the Core Self

The Core Self is our essence. It is who we are at the most fundamental level. It includes all the gifts and talents we possess in their potential. It is what makes us unique. It is the blueprint we are born with.

All of us have a Core Self, but not many of us are in touch with it. That is because the Core Self can be encountered only with unconditional love and acceptance. If we look without love and acceptance, we will not see the Core Self. We will see the Wounded Self. The Wounded Self grows up with conditional love and lives in a state of fear.

The Core Self cannot be injured or hurt by any of our experiences. That is because it is whole and complete. There is nothing lacking in it. There is nothing in it that needs to be changed or fixed.

When we are connected to our Core Self, we are connected to all that is. We live in relationship to our Source or higher power. We abide in who we are.

The Core Self is our energetic connection to Love. It connects us heart to heart to each other. When we rest in the Core Self, there is no separation. There are no separate bodies or separate agendas. There is just infinite, boundless love.

The Core Self is there, even though we have not encountered it. It cannot be destroyed or taken away from us. However, it can be disguised, covered over or ignored. And it can take some of us a very long time to remove those disguises and come face to face with our essence.

Use the space below to journal your experience with your Core Self. When have you felt the connection to your essence most intensely? Do you do any kind of spiritual practice that helps you to connect with your Core Self on a daily basis?

∞ Journal Notes ∞

The Wounded Self

The Core Self is usually overshadowed by the Wounded Self. That is because we are all carrying a great deal of shame and unworthiness. We are all living in the shadows of our wound.

How do we know we are wounded? We know because we have anger in our hearts. We feel less than or better than others. We judge and attack others or we beat up on ourselves. We feel overwhelmed by feelings of grief, jealousy, or unworthiness. We are triggered in our relationships. We have reactive behavior. We fight with others or run away from them.

We know that we are wounded because there is a lot of fear that comes up and we don't know how to hold that fear compassionately. We don't know how to be with our fear or the fear of others.

We know that we are wounded because we can't find peace in our hearts or in our relationships. In addition, we may have memories of a traumatic event that altered our life such as rape, incest, physical abuse, the death of a parent or another experience of abandonment or betrayal.

Many of the exercises in this book will help you get in touch with your wounds. For now, please journal any awareness you have about your Wounded Self.

∽ Journal Notes ∽

31

Shadow and Persona

Because we stuff our pain, part of our experience and the emotions associated with it is repressed and locked away.

The psyche is split in two. The part that we don't want to see or feel is called the shadow and the part that we accept is called the persona.

The shadow includes the early childhood experiences that were too traumatic for us to process consciously. It includes all our fears and demons that run our lives at an unconscious level.

The persona is that aspect of self that we are comfortable with and allow others to see. We keep developing our persona (our mask) in order to win the acceptance and approval that we want from others. We believe that if we can hide our pain, then people will find us more attractive, worthy, and lovable.

Each of us has both a shadow and a persona. The shadow is the "bad" or "dark" side of us. The persona is the "good" or "bright" side of us. Actually, neither shadow nor persona is an accurate representation of who we are. They are both distortions of self. Only when the two are integrated and the psyche returns to wholeness do we begin to get a realistic sense of who we are.

Use the space below to describe your shadow and your persona. You may also find it helpful to draw pictures of them or cut out and paste pictures from magazines and newspapers that evoke your shadow self or your mask/persona.

❧ Journal Notes ❧

The Mask that Hides our Pain

In our desire for acceptance and approval from others, some of us learn to contrive very sophisticated masks. They fit around us so tightly we can hardly breathe.

Yet no matter how good the mask, it eventually cracks or wears thin. Denial cannot last forever. Eventually, our wound begins to bleed through. The disguise no longer works and we feel scared and exposed.

It isn't easy to admit that we have failed to live behind our mask. What we don't realize is that everyone fails. All masks fall away. The wound can and must reveal itself.

It seems strange that some of us would rather die than admit how much we hurt. But that is how deep our shame is. And that is how hard it is to tell the truth when we live in a culture of denial.

This work of emotional healing asks you to do something very courageous. It asks you to remove your mask and get in touch with your pain and your shame. It asks you to acknowledge your wound and bring love to it.

It is not easy for any of us to come face to face with our pain. But it is the doorway to real healing and transformation. Please use the space below to journal about your fear of removing your mask and facing your pain. In which areas of your life have you successfully removed your mask? In which areas is your mask still intact?

∞ Journal Notes ∞

The False Self and the Wounded Child

Our False Self is the collection of all the masks that we wear at home, at work, and in our community. Many of our masks are developed so that we can pretend to be well adjusted adults with important roles and responsibilities. Of course, underneath the adult mask is the scared little kid who isn't ready to grow up and take responsibility.

As a child, we just want to be loved and accepted without conditions, but as we grow into adulthood we learn to buy into the demands of conditional love. We learn to show up to please others. We learn to do what we are expected to do.

Unfortunately, the bargain we made is not fulfilled. Conditional love does not pay off. The little kid within us never gets the love and acceptance he thought he would get. He has sacrificed himself without getting payback. He has betrayed himself for nothing.

Is it any wonder that he is on the warpath?

This amounts to a real psychological crisis. That child is going to start to demand love. He is no longer going to be willing to live in sacrifice or behave himself. His selfishness is going to shine through. His behavior might no longer be pretty or socially acceptable.

He might even turn into a monster, a raving lunatic, a Tasmanian devil. This is the shadow side erupting. It usually isn't very pleasant. However, it is a necessary event in the transformation of the psyche.

The shadow can no longer be held back by the persona. The mask must be ripped off.

The energy that has been trapped in self betrayal must be released. The division in the psyche must be vitiated so that darkness can connect with light and integration can occur.

Please use the space below to consider how your wounded child is doing. Is s/he hidden behind the mask of the False Self or is s/he clamoring for attention? Is s/he patiently waiting for others to deliver on the promise of love, or is s/he angry and restless?

∞ Journal Notes ∞

The Death of the False Self

The eruption of the shadow is a sign that the False Self is gradually losing its grip.

Holes appear in its armor. The outer skin—once perfectly made up—becomes wrinkled and blemished. The hair—once neatly cut and permed—becomes ragged and disheveled.

For some people, the False Self slowly degrades and dissolves as they move to honor themselves. For others who hold onto self-betrayal at all cost, the False Self falls off the wall like Humpty Dumpty, shattering into thousands of pieces.

For some, the death of the False Self may require being locked up in a detox facility or a psychiatric hospital. For others it might involve watching their marriage fall apart or being fired from a job that has become their identity.

The death of the False Self is hardly ever painless or pretty. We all cling to some degree to our old, self-limiting images, beliefs, roles and responsibilities. As a result, they have to be dislodged or wrestled away from this. Shiva must come with his sword and cut away our attachments to the past, so that we can be reborn into a new, more empowered life.

The fire that consumes the past must burn until nothing limiting remains. Then the phoenix can rise from the ashes. Then the True Self can be born.

Use the space below to describe your experience with the dissolution, degradation and eventual death of your False Self.

∞ Journal Notes ∞

35

Spiritual Awakening

The birth of the True Self is often called a spiritual awakening experience. For many of us, though, it is not just a single experience, but a series of important experiences. It is a process that requires us to throw away our mask and begin to look at our fear, our shame, and our hurt. It asks us to go willingly into the darkness of our psyche to reclaim the light. In so doing, we are able to encounter our unworthiness and transform it.

Many spiritual students try to skip over this step on their journey, but it does not work. Lest we heal our wounds, we cannot encounter the Core Self. And until we encounter our Core Self, we cannot learn how to be true to it.

The True Self is born when the False Self dies and we come face to face with our essence. Then, we can no longer betray ourselves. Then, everything we think, feel, say and do gradually comes into alignment with who we are. That is when we step fully into our power and life purpose.

Please use the space below to describe your spiritual awakening experiences and how they are leading you to see and be true to your Core Self.

⚮ Journal Notes ⚮

Core Self and True Self

The False Self betrays the Core Self. The True Self honors the Core Self.

The Core Self is not really of this world. It is of the heavenly realm. It is in our heart of hearts. It is our essence.

The True Self is the expression of the Core Self in the world. It is in the world, but not of the world.

All of our talents and gifts exist as potential in the Core Self. They are developed and expressed by our True Self. The True Self is the engine of our creative expression. Because it is aligned with the Core Self, the True Self is energy incarnate. It harnesses the kundalini energy and puts it to work in our lives.

The Core Self is a noun, an essence, a potential. The True Self is a verb. It is action, movement, fulfillment.

The Core Self is nurtured by Divine Mother. Her work is all about helping us love and accept ourselves just the way we are. The True Self is empowered by Divine Father. His work is all about helping us discover and express our creative gifts.

The Core Self is about Being. The True Self is about Doing.

Doing must always be in alignment with Being or it will be wrong-doing. All the work of the False Self is wrong-doing. It is action without heart. It is all about trespass and betrayal.

When Doing comes into alignment with Being, action is heartfelt. It honors self and others. This leads to right doing, right livelihood, right relationship.

When the True Self asserts itself, we are reborn in integrity. We become authentic and naturally align with our spiritual purpose. We live not from the outside in, but from the inside out. Our life is no longer driven by fear and run by our ego. It is inspired by love and directed by the indwelling Spirit that makes its home in our Core Self.

Please use the space below to reflect on how Being and Doing are in alignment in your life. Are you being true to yourself and expressing the gifts and talents you were born with?

---

೦೦ Journal Notes ೦೦

37

PART 4

Opening Our Hearts
to Healing

The Symptoms & Causes of Unhappiness

It is important for each one of us to discover both the symptoms and the causes of our unhappiness. Sometimes identifying the symptom of our unhappiness can help us identify the wound that causes it. Please read through the list below and check the boxes that apply to you. Please add to the list as necessary.

❒ Feeling guilty about my past

❒ Unable to forgive myself

❒ Shame about physical/emotional/sexual abuse

❒ Being highly critical toward myself or others

❒ Feeling unworthy/lack of self esteem

❒ Lack of self-confidence or fear of failure

❒ High levels of anxiety or stress

❒ Laziness, lack of motivation, goals or purpose

❒ Needing to blame others for my problems

❒ Unable to forgive the trespasses of others

❒ Infidelity/sex addiction, workaholism

❒ Persistent financial problems, obsession with money

❒ Acting impulsively or irresponsibly

❒ Suicidal or homicidal thoughts

❒ Abusing drugs/alcohol or other substances

❒ Feeling fearful or paranoid

❒ Constant stream of negative thoughts

❒ Post Traumatic Stress Disorder

❒ Schizophrenia, Psychosis or other mental illness

❒ Chronic fatigue, lack of energy

❒ Feeling lost, powerless or helpless

❒ Feeling depressed, lack of meaning in my life

❒ _____

❒ _____

❒ _____

✌ Journal Notes ✌

Check the conditions that apply to you and ask yourself, "Is this a symptom of my unhappiness or a cause of it?" If you feel that you have identified a cause of your unhappiness, ask yourself, "What is the origin of this?" Also ask, "Do any others in my family have this condition?" Keep inquiring into the origin of the condition so that you will begin to map the territory of your pain and move closer to an awareness of your core wound. Document your insights in the space below.

The Dominant Emotion

The dominant emotion is the way that you are feeling most of the time. Below are some examples of dominant emotions. Check the boxes that apply and/or add to the list as necessary.

- ☐ Sad
- ☐ Envious
- ☐ Anxious
- ☐ Worried
- ☐ Manic

- ☐ Angry
- ☐ Hurt
- ☐ Fearful
- ☐ Depressed
- ☐ Paranoid

☐ _____   ☐ _____
☐ _____   ☐ _____

Your dominant emotion is the doorway to your core wound and your core belief about yourself. Your dominant emotion will usually be quite obvious to others who are close to you. So if you don't know what it is, ask your spouse, your children, or your coworkers.

Please use the journal space below to record your observations.

∞ Journal Notes ∞

The Core Wound

Each one of us has many wounds. Some are superficial. Some are deep. Some are recent. Some go way back to our childhood or perhaps even in utero. In some cases, we may even be carrying ancestral wounds that go back to previous generations.

One way into our pain is to ask, "What hurts most right now?" For example, perhaps three months ago your marriage fell apart and your spouse moved out of the house. That's the recent wound. But behind that wound will be another. For instance, perhaps you married a critical woman like your mother. So not only are you experiencing the break up of your marriage, you are also experiencing your mommy wound.

Moreover, your oldest child may be acting out by taking drugs and skipping school, rebelling against mommy just like you did when you were younger. The severity of your anger at him may surprise you until you realize that your son's actions are triggering your core wound.

All our wounds can be traced back to a core wound. Understanding that core wound and your reaction to it is extremely important if you are going to heal your pain.

Use the journal space below to begin exploring your core wound. Ask yourself "What hurts most right now?" and "What old hurt does this recent hurt remind me of?"

∞ Journal Notes ∞

Mother and Father Wounds

∞ Journal Notes ∞

The Core Wound may be inflicted by mommy, by daddy, by a sibling, by another family member or by a significant other. Some wounds can be inflicted by a total stranger, or simply by life or fate.

There are mother wounds and father wounds. A *mommy wound* involves too much, too little, or inappropriate attention from mommy. A *daddy wound* involves too much, too little, or inappropriate attention from daddy.

Most of us have a mommy wound and a daddy wound. Often the mommy and daddy wound run together as in the case where we have a critical, controlling mother and a weak or absent father. In other words, too much mommy often means too little daddy and vice versa

In the adjoining journal space please identify your mommy wound and your daddy wound. On the next page you will find some examples of Core Wounds.

Examples of Core Wounds

Please check the box next to the wounds that apply to you and highlight for emphasis. Add to the list as necessary.

- ☐ Abandonment (physical and emotional). Includes death or illness of parents or their unavailability because of divorce, active military service, addiction to drugs or alcohol.

- ☐ Betrayal (trust established, then betrayed). Includes ambivalence or emotional instability of caretakers including the mental or physical illness of parents.

- ☐ Abuse (physical, emotional, sexual, or ritual)

- ☐ Incest (emotional, sexual). Includes lack of appropriate boundaries or inappropriate behavior by parents, siblings or other family members.

- ☐ Confinement, imprisonment, control

- ☐ Lack of limits/too much freedom

- ☐ Stolen childhood/caretaking of parents or siblings (being forced to take on adult responsibilities before we are ready)

- ☐ Pampering, spoiling, low expectations, overprotection

- ☐ Danger/lack of safety (physical or emotional)

- ☐ Guilt, false responsibility (for a parent or sibling's death or illness, etc)

- ☐ Birth Trauma, birth defects, premature birth

- ☐ Serious or extensive illness in childhood

- ☐ Not being wanted, unplanned pregnancy

- ☐ Rejection by a parent, post-partum depression of mother

- ☐ Persecution by siblings

- ☐ Repeated humiliation, criticism, shaming, blaming by parents or significant others

- ☐ _____

- ☐ _____

Journal Notes

Take some time to journal about your core wound and core beliefs. The healing process requires that you identify where you hurt the most and what beliefs lurk in your subconscious and run your life.

Our Core Beliefs

Journal Notes

Take some time to journal about your core wound and core beliefs. The healing process requires that you identify where you hurt the most and what beliefs lurk in your subconscious and run your life.

Our Core Belief about ourselves is created out of the shame or unworthiness attached to our Core Wound. Our Core Belief drives our experience of ourselves and the world. All Core Beliefs can be summed up by this one: "I am not worthy of love."

Below are some other examples of Core Beliefs. Check the boxes for all of the Core Beliefs that belong to you. Highlight the ones that are most important. If you do not see your Core Belief, please add it to the list.

❒ Nothing I do is good enough.

❒ I'm a bad or evil person (or I would not have been beaten/sexually abused).

❒ I am unworthy. I don't deserve to breathe the air.

❒ I am a failure. I will never amount to anything.

❒ I am stupid. Others are smarter than I am.

❒ I have to be smarter than others to be loved.

❒ I am unattractive.

❒ I am weak or sickly.

❒ I am unlikable, awkward, foolish, etc.

❒ I am unlovable.

❒ The world is not a safe place. If I am not careful, I will be hurt.

❒ I show up for others, but no one shows up for me.

❒ Love is too scary. I am better off alone.

❒ I can't do it by myself. Someone else must do it for me.

❒ I have to do it by myself. No one else can help.

❒ My needs do not matter. I have to take care of others (mommy, daddy, etc.).

❒ Whatever I do, it won't be enough.

❒ When I trust the universe, I get smashed.

❒ If I stand up for myself, I won't be loved.

Reactive Behavior Pattern

Our reactive behavior pattern is the way that we react when fear comes up. Some of us respond to fear by internalizing it (stuffing it) and some of us respond by externalizing it (projecting it onto others).

If we have an *Inward Reaction Pattern,* we try to hide from others or become invisible when we get scared. We become physically or emotionally inaccessible, self absorbed or obsessed. We run away or disappear. We don't confront others. We internalize our anger. We blame ourselves. We become a victim.

If we have an *Outward Reaction Pattern,* we attack others when fear comes up. Our behavior is emotionally or physically intrusive, aggressive, or overbearing. We are verbally or physically abusive. We yell, hit, blame and shame. We express our anger without owning it or looking at it. We become a victimizer.

Generally, we tend to copy the reactive behavior pattern of our dominant parent and to attract relationships with people who have the opposite behavior pattern, thus reliving the psycho-dynamics of our parents' relationship. We must become conscious of these dynamics and our part in them if we are going to change them. Otherwise, the dynamics will be reinforced and we will pass these patterns on to our children.

Use the adjoining journal space to identify and elaborate on your reactive behavior pattern. Note how it has operated in the past and how it operates now. To what extent have you recognized this pattern and taken steps to change it?"

❧ Journal Notes ❧

Life Lessons

Each one of us comes into this life with certain lessons that we must learn. There are qualities that we need to develop in order to find greater balance in our lives.

Our reactive behavior patterns stemming from our core wound and our core belief about ourselves often push us into too much introversion or extroversion. We need to bring balance.

Introverts need to learn to reach out to others, interact with people and get feedback. Extroverts need to take time alone to connect with themselves, get in touch with their feelings, and understand what is really important to them.

Use the space below to reflect on how you can learn your lessons and bring balance to your life.

∽ Journal Notes ∽

Mapping Your Wound/Strategies for Healing

If you want real happiness in your life, you must understand your mental/emotional triggers and the reactive patterns of behavior that originate in your childhood. If you don't understand your core wound and your core belief about yourself, you will continue to be unconsciously driven by them. You will be like a marionette being controlled by hidden strings that jerk you around when you least expect it.

How can you take charge of your life if you don't understand how you hurt and where your pain originates? You must learn to see the psychological structure of your suffering so that you can heal your pain and step into your power.

By answering the questions that follow, you will create a map of your wound and your strategies for healing.

Please use additional paper to answer these questions in depth. Take your time and be as thorough as you can be. If you find it helpful, do this process with a friend and/or a therapist and share your story. You may find that it is helpful to do this exercise several times over the next year. Each time you sit down to do it, you will have new understandings and revelations about yourself.

Be sure to answer in depth questions eight and nine (lessons/strategies for healing). Your answers to these questions amount to a prescription for happiness and give you concrete homework to do over the next year.

๑ Journal Notes ๑

1. What is the *dominant emotion* that permeates your consciousness?

2. What is your *core wound?* Who hurt you and how did they hurt you?

3. What is your *core belief?* What is the message about yourself you internalized?

4. What is your *reactive behavior pattern?* How did you react to the wound/hurt?

5. How can you reverse your *reactive behavior pattern?*

6. What are your *present triggers?* How does this behavior pattern show up in your life and your relationships now?

7. What is the *chain of abuse?* How are your reactive behavior patterns impacting your children or other loved ones? How is your core wound being passed on?

8. What are the *lessons* you need to learn?

9. What *strategies for healing* can help you learn these lessons and transform your life?

Example Worksheet

1. *Dominant emotion:* Sad and depressed. I see that I beat myself up constantly.

2. *Core Wound(s):* Daddy was not present. Mommy was highly critical.

3. *Core Belief:* Nothing I do is good enough. I am a failure.

4. *Reactive Pattern:* Flight, introversion, isolating, becoming inaccessible, blaming and shaming myself.

5. *How this pattern shows up in my life:* I married a woman like my mother who was highly critical of me. That exacerbated my mother wound. I couldn't stand up to my mother or my wife. I ran away. I am now divorced.

6. *How my wound is being passed on:* I love my children, but I see that, like my father, I am often an absent parent. I am absorbed in my work, which is not very fulfilling. I also see that I have become a critical parent like my mother. I expect a lot from my children. It is hard for me to love them unconditionally.

7. *Lessons/Strategies for Healing:* Learn to stand up to my mother and stop trying to win her approval. Learn to be my own mother and love myself unconditionally. Love and accept my children as they are. Stop trying to prove myself and win the approval of the women in my life. Look for positive male role models, especially older men, who will encourage me and embody the father energy I didn't have growing up. Learn to take the pressure off and be more gentle with myself. Stop working so hard and being so serious. Lighten up and take time to enjoy my life. Be childlike. Learn to trust, to play, to be spontaneous.

8. *Reversal of Reactive Pattern:* Stop running away when I am scared.

A Roadmap of the Healing Process

Below you will find a simple roadmap for the process of emotional healing. Read through each step below and evaluate your progress on the journey. Be honest. Give yourself credit for what you have learned and be clear on the challenges that lie ahead.

1 *Accept the wound.* It happened to you. It is part of your life. You are not going to make it go away. *My Progress:*

2 *Remove the Shame.* Whatever happened, you must come to see that it was not your fault. You were innocent. Stop blaming yourself. There is nothing wrong or bad about you. *My Progress:*

3 *Acknowledge your pain and share it with others.* Stop running away from the pain or trying to hide it. Get into therapy. Get help with your addictions so that you meet the pain head-on. Share your pain with others. You are not the only one who has been hurt in this way. Find a healing community where you can give and receive support and empowerment to heal and become whole. *My Progress:*

4. *Confront and forgive your abuser.* If there are words that you need to say and you can say them, do so. If the opportunity isn't there to look your abuser in the eye, write a letter or talk into a tape recorder. Get out all of the anger and hurt. Don't hold onto it anymore. It doesn't belong to you. Scream, hit, beat a pillow, let the pain go. When you are done, burn that letter or that recording. Forgive your abuser. Keep forgiving whenever the opportunity arises. There are many layers of pain and you must bring forgiveness to each one of them. *My Progress:*

5. *Stop being a victim.* Drop your story. Stop shaming and blaming yourself or others. Get on with your life. Let the old life go. Start creating a new life. *My Progress:*

6. *Create a support system,* a spiritual family that understands where you have come from and where you are going. Make new friends. Find mentors and positive role models to emulate. *My Progress:*

7. *Embrace your gifts* and begin to give them. If those gifts need refinement, take a class or two. Apprentice yourself to a master. Develop your skills and talents so that you can offer your gifts freely and confidently. Everyone has something to offer. Focus on what is joyful to you and comes naturally without great effort. Take some creative risks. Fulfill your potential. Discover your life purpose. That is what you are here for. *My Progress:*

9. *Empower people to make their own decisions* and to take charge of their lives. Don't become responsible for others or try to carry them through life. Teach them to be responsible for themselves and to get on with their lives, as you did. *My Progress:*

8. *Help others heal.* Give back to those who are scared and wounded as you once were. Be a facilitator and a role model. Offer people hope that healing is possible. *My Progress:*

As a general rule, our wounds heal as we learn to accept and love ourselves unconditionally. All of the steps in the roadmap contribute to that goal. As love flows to the wounded places within, they begin to heal and we begin to feel stronger and more whole. Forgiveness of self and others becomes easier and goes deeper. We let go of our shame and blame and learn to be gentle with ourselves and others.

PART 5

Finding, Trusting
and Expressing Our Gifts

Discovering Your Gift

Your Core Self is the jewel-like spark of light that you have come here to nurture, to empower, and to shine upon the world. Your Core Self always bears a gift that you must discover and learn to give. This gift includes the skills, talents, abilities and strengths you come into this life with. They come naturally to you and their expression is both joyful and effortless.

Usually you have to go through a process of nurturing and refining the gift and then learning to trust it. This process is essential if you are to find real happiness in your life. If your gifts are unused or forgotten, you will not harvest the joy and fulfillment that are your birthright. The universe did its part by giving you that bright light within your heart of hearts. Your job is to find the light and learn to shine it.

Remember that your gift is not just for you. It is for everyone. The expression of your gift not only brings joy to you; it also brings joy to others. It serves your well-being, as well as the greater good of humankind.

Once you know what your gift is and become confident in your ability to give it, you are provided with opportunities to share it. The more you share it and walk through the open doors, the more doors will open to you. Gradually, you will step into your life purpose. You will know what you are here on the planet to do and nothing will bring you greater joy or fulfillment than this.

There are many types of gifts. Here are some of them:

- *Creative Gifts* (entertaining/uplifting others by singing, dancing, painting, writing, playing music, acting)

- *Emotional Gifts* (nurturing, support, optimism, encouragement, enthusiasm, spontaneity)

- *Physical Gifts* (athleticism, coordination, stamina, strength, agility, vitality, longevity)

- *Intellectual Gifts* (powers of memory, logic, analysis, discrimination, clear thinking)

- *Psychic Gifts* (prophecy, telepathy, empathy, intuition, clairaudience, clairvoyance)

- *Spiritual Gifts* (understanding, compassion, acceptance, faith, trust, peace, joy, oneness)

Below is a list of some of the gifts possessed by people in our community. Please review the list and check the boxes that apply to you. If you can't find one of your gifts there, please add it to the list. Then answer the questions that follow. They will help you understand where you stand in relationship to nurturing, developing and expressing each of your gifts.

- ❐ the gift of surrender
- ❐ the gift of forgiveness
- ❐ the gift of healing
- ❐ the gift of acceptance
- ❐ the gift of responsibility
- ❐ the gift of caring
- ❐ the gift of non-blaming communication
- ❐ the gift of devotional singing/chanting
- ❐ the gift of writing
- ❐ the gift of public speaking
- ❐ the gift of facilitating
- ❐ the gift of yoga, tai chi, qi gong, paneurhythmy
- ❐ the gift of painting, sculpture, photography
- ❐ the gift of listening
- ❐ the gift of nurturing and supporting
- ❐ the gift of teaching, coaching and mentoring
- ❐ the gift of manifesting
- ❐ the gift of discernment/discrimination
- ❐ the gift of compassion
- ❐ the gift of cooperation/co-creating
- ❐ the gift of gratitude
- ❐ the gift of creating sacred space/ritual
- ❐ the gift of connecting people/networking

೦ಅ Journal Notes ೦ಅ

In the space below, please add any of your gifts that you don't see on the previous list.

Now please answer the following questions:

1. Do you accept and embrace your gift?

2. Have you taken the time to develop and refine your gift?

3. Are you currently trusting your gift and offering it to others?

If the answer to any of these questions is "No," please ask yourself three more questions:

1. What stands in the way of your acknowledging, accepting, and embracing your gift?

2. What stops you from developing/refining your gift?

3. What prevents you from actively sharing your gift with others?

Focus on What You Want to Create

Whatever you dwell on, whatever you give your energy and attention to, whatever you invest your emotion in, tends to grow. So consider wisely what you focus on.

Spend your time thinking about what you want to create, not thinking about what you want to avoid. Look forward to the things that you enjoy. Don't fixate on the things that you hate.

After you have embraced your pain and looked at your dysfunctional patterns, you must shift gears. You must leave the old, fragmented self behind and let the new, integrated self be born. Like the emerging butterfly, you must shed your old caterpillar skin and let your new multi-colored wings emerge.

Don't get attached to your pain. Let the old story go and begin to create a new story.

Don't get attached to your wound. Allow it to heal.

Don't be content to be a victim. Victims don't heal.

Be a Creator of your own life. Take your power back and take charge of your life. It is both your right and your responsibility to exercise your free will.

Here is an exercise that you might find helpful. Sit down at the beginning of the week and take five or ten minutes to be silent and ask yourself these questions:

- What do I want to create in my life this week? What are my goals for this week?

- What actions am I willing to take to move forward toward achieving my goals?

Write the answers to these questions in the journal space below. Read your answers every day when you get up in the morning. Stay aligned with the goals you have set and the action commitments you have made. If unanticipated obstacles arise, see them as challenges. Notice the adjustment that is being required and write it into your action plan for the following week.

Part of what life teaches us is how to be strong and determined. You can't achieve much in life if you give up too easily. All human beings need to learn both patience and persistence.

Having low expectations for ourselves or for other people does not help. Shooting too low and shooting too high amount to the same thing. Both miss the mark.

The trick is to set realistic goals and work diligently to achieve them. That is a surefire recipe for success.

ဆ Journal Notes ဆ

Discover Your House of Healing

Many of us are looking all over the globe for our life purpose when it is right under our nose. When we reach out to help someone who needs our help, our purpose is made clear. We are here to heal and to help others heal. It's not any more esoteric or complicated than that.

You started your journey to wholeness by acknowledging and healing your wound. You learned to forgive yourself and others for the pain of the past. You learned to move beyond victim consciousness and to take charge of your life. You are the living proof that healing and reconciliation are possible.

Right now, in your town or city, others are struggling with the same core wound. They are still blaming and shaming themselves and others. Or they are in denial of their wound, trying to lose themselves in work, sex, drugs or alcohol. You know what it means to be in denial because you have been there. You know what it means to shame and blame because you did these things too. Who else is going to reach out to these people?

You may say, "Well, that's not my responsibility." And you are right; it is not your responsibility. It is their responsibility to heal. But, as a practical matter, only a small number of them are going to heal by themselves. If it weren't for you, they wouldn't find the doorway. They would keep going through the same old doors. They would continue to walk down the same dead-end streets. They would stay in their pain.

But you know how they feel and the way that they think. They won't listen to others, but they will listen to you. Whether or not you believe in God, you cannot close your eyes to the suffering of your fellow human beings. You cannot help but feel their pain. You cannot hear their cry for help and turn away from them.

It's an old but true adage that when the teacher is ready, the students show up. When you are ready to give back, those who need to receive your gift will find you. It's truly awesome. It is a powerful demonstration that there is a spiritual reality at work in our lives. When we are engaged in helping others to heal, we know at long last that we are in our "right place" in this world.

Use the space below to describe your house of healing and the ways in which your gifts can be used to help facilitate healing for others with wounds that are similar to your own.

∞ Journal Notes ∞

Understand the Law of Attraction

Why do we try to manifest our dreams and fail? Because we are creating from our Wounded Self, not from our Core Self. Until we heal our wounds, we cannot manifest our gift or give it to others. Until we heal our pain, all we will do is recreate it over and over again.

Until we find out who we are and what we really want, we are going to create suffering. It's that simple. For the Law of Attraction to work, we must create through our connection with our Core Self. That means that we are creating out of the awareness that we are loved and we are worthy. Below you will find some common misunderstandings about this law to avoid. Please take the time to journal on those you find most relevant.

Misunderstanding #1: I create what I want.

True if you are connected to your Core Self. Wrong if you aren't. Your False Self will create what you don't want and don't need.

Misunderstanding #2: I know what I want.

Think again. Most people haven't got the slightest idea what they want. They have just borrowed ideas from their parents and other authority figures. Sometimes it is better to get clear on what you don't want and see what's left over.

Misunderstanding #3: I am here to help others.

Yes, that's true. But first you need to help yourself and heal your own wounds. Until you do that, you won't be very helpful to others.

Misunderstanding #4: I can manifest all the money I desire.

Well, maybe. Some people are good at business and finance. Some are not. Even those who are good at it aren't necessarily happy. If you have trouble making ends meet, or you are doing a job that you hate to do, money might not be the real issue. Your problem might be that you are out of alignment with your Core Self and your creative gifts.

Misunderstanding #5: I can have the perfect relationship.

It will be the "perfect" relationship to push your buttons and make you aware of all the healing you still need to do. All relationships are learning laboratories. You inevitably attract a partner who has the same level of love and fear that you have. As a result, you mirror each other and there are plenty of opportunities to learn, to grow, and to heal.

∞ Journal Notes ∞

Discover Your Passion

To act without a passion for what we are doing leads to self-betrayal. That is why we must connect with the heart and find our passion. If we don't, what we do will not satisfy.

We live in a world that is imbalanced. The beliefs that support that imbalance are simple ones and need to be challenged.

1. I must do something (even if I don't want to).

Please question this belief. Often it is better to do nothing than to do something out of anxiety, boredom, or the anticipated criticism of the authority figures in your life.

2. If I don't do something, I will starve and become homeless.

Don't let your fear push you into a panic. Not doing is undertaken not as a permanent solution, but as a break from doing what we know is not working. It is a time to center, to observe, to get perspective, to receive guidance or inspiration. In other words, it is a way of bringing in the Divine Mother energy when we really need it.

3. Doing more is better than doing less.

This is true only if what you are doing is working and is in harmony with your life. If it is not working or in harmony, doing less is better.

If we question these erroneous beliefs and assumptions, we can begin to bring balance into our lives. We can slow down, connect to our hearts, and begin to do things that we really care about and can be committed to. That way we will learn to create enthusiastically and responsibly. We won't act impulsively and betray ourselves or others, nor will we procrastinate or make promises we can't keep.

Please comment in the journal space below on which beliefs are most relevant for you and consider how you can begin to challenge them.

∞ Journal Notes ∞

PART 6

Joyful Practices

Develop Witness Consciousness

Healing requires a commitment to daily spiritual practice. One practice that can be helpful is taking 20–30 minutes each day simply getting quiet and watching your thoughts.

When you watch your thoughts, you detach from them and become the witness. You notice the thoughts that come and go in your mind, but you do not hold onto them or try to push them away. You remain neutral and just notice what is happening.

If you find yourself identifying with a particular thought or with an emotion attached to it, you simply notice that and remind yourself that you are an observer, not a participant.

In the beginning of this practice, you believe that your thoughts belong to you. But after a period of witnessing your thoughts, you begin to see them as just thoughts, not as *your* thoughts. You are no longer identifying with your thoughts. They are not you.

The same thing begins to happen with the emotions that are attached to these thoughts. They become just feelings, not *your* feelings. So when sadness comes up, at first it is your sadness about the fact that your mom died when you were six. But after a while, it is just "sadness," or "story about sadness."

The beauty of witness consciousness is that it holds us up above the wound so that we can look at it without identifying with it. This is very helpful.

From this place, we can see how easy it is to get attached to our story. We can see how we want to make that story our identity. We can see how easy it is for us to claim the role of victim and start making hundreds of excuses for why we cannot change anything in our life.

The wonderful thing here is that the witness who sees "the victim" cannot be the victim. That is the gift of awareness. When we are aware of a pattern, we can't be in that pattern.

Experiment cultivating witness consciousness and keep a record here of any insights it leads you to.

∞ Journal Notes ∞

Give Thanks and Celebrate

We experience joy when we celebrate and give thanks. When we open our mouths to chant the words of love or to sing songs of celebration, we experience joy, ecstasy, bliss.

When we dance the dances of gratitude and peace, our hearts open and we feel energy moving through our hands and feet. When we bless others, when we bless ourselves, we are uplifted and so are they. When we volunteer to help someone who needs our help, we feel goodness and grace all around us.

The human spirit was meant to dance, to sing, to celebrate life. It craves this expression and cannot do without it.

Recognizing this, one way to cultivate joy in your life is to take the time each week to gather with others to celebrate the good in life and give thanks for your blessings. Join a chorus, meet people from all traditions who dance the Dances of Universal Peace, spend an evening chanting, praying or drumming. Rituals like these nourish the heart. And, in our culture, the heart is not often nourished.

There is so much in our lives that brings us down, scares us and worries us. Every time we turn on the television or read the newspaper, we are besieged by negative news about people being raped, murdered, or killed. This saddens our hearts and eats away at our hope.

You cannot keep feeding your heart poison or it will shrivel up and die. You need to feed it nourishing food. It needs to hear the good news, not just the bad news. It needs to hear about miracles, not just about disasters.

Just as you choose what you put in your mouth, you also choose what you feed your heart and your mind, and the hearts and minds of your children.

Don't settle for violence and cruelty. Don't be content with the bad news. Don't go through life complaining about all the terrible things that happen in the world. Find the good things. Bring them into your heart and your home. Celebrate them with your children.

Be the one who brings hope, not the one who brings despair. Be the one who celebrates, not the one who complains. Be the one who brings love, not the one who invokes fear.

This week try an experiment. Change your mental and emotional diet. Turn off the TV. Put the electronic paraphernalia away. Turn off the cell phones, the computers, the video games. Take a break from the human obsession with motors and machines.

Celebrate the Sabbath old-style. Don't even get in your car. Take your children and spouse by the hand and take a long walk by the river, through the woods or in the park. Spend time with each other. Look into each other's eyes. Be grateful for the time you have with each other. Life will be over in the blink of an eye. Don't miss the opportunity to express your love and your gratitude.

Keep a record of your experience in your journal. If you have a good experience, you can extend your practice or build some aspects of it into your daily lifestyle.

∾ Journal Notes ∾

Give Up Negativity

This practice asks you to give up complaining or being negative cold turkey. It challenges you to take every event and circumstance in your life that pushes your buttons and find a way to respond to it positively. That means that there will be times when you just have to override your doubt, your fear, or your skepticism and find a way to affirm what is happening. Find something good in it to celebrate. Find the strand of hope, however small and inconspicuous it may be, and call attention to it.

Pretend that you have just been appointed anchor of the NBC or CBS news and have been given Carte Blanche on the news that you are going to report. Report the good news. And if you feel you have to report the bad news too, report it in a positive and hopeful way.

People need to know that happiness is possible. They are hungry for empowerment and you choose to empower them. Sure, you know that healing and empowerment are a process and don't happen overnight. But you are going to encourage them to hang in there.

You aren't denying the pain. You are bringing salve and dressing for the wounds. You are affirming the value of life and supporting the will to live, to learn and to transform pain and fear into acceptance and love.

Try this practice for a day and see what happens. If you are brave, try it for a whole week. Keep a record of the results in this journal space below.

∞ Journal Notes ∞

Rise Above the Drama

Shakespeare told us: "All the world's a stage, and all the men and women merely players."

Life is 95 percent drama, and 5 percent essence. That means that we live primarily in the drama. We take things very seriously and spend the majority of our time reacting unconsciously to the events and circumstances of our lives.

If we could step off the stage for a moment and watch the drama unfolding, we would realize how absurd it is. We would see that we make life much harder and more complicated than it needs to be.

When we rise above the drama, we can see what the essence is and attend to it. We can let the rest just slide off our shoulders. We learn to focus on what is really important and not to sweat the small stuff. Then, even the sharks turn into minnows.

Each one of us must find a way to get off the stage and see what's happening there from a more transcendent perspective. Otherwise, we become mired in the muck of life and it's hard to find clarity or peace.

There are many ways to do this. For some people, meditation works. Taking a long walk every day can serve the same purpose. When we walk up in the mountains, by a stream or on a deserted beach, far away from human sights and sounds, we recharge physically, emotionally, mentally, and spiritually. Personally, I find it is impossible to be depressed, agitated or self-obsessed when I am surrounded by towering trees, rushing water, wind or surf. The sounds of nature calm my body, cleanse my mind, uplift my emotions, and awaken my spirit. As I walk, I breathe deeply and let go of the demands and pressures of my life. I remember who I really am and reconnect to my Core Self. Then I return to my human life more centered and clear about what is really important.

Each of us must find some kind of daily ritual that helps us move our energy out of our head and into the rest of our body. Otherwise, we become imbalanced and begin to get stressed out. The following questions will help you make a list of some of the ways that you can rise above the drama.

- What rituals help you to slow things down, let go of the small stuff, and see what's really important?

- What rituals help you lower your stress levels, balance the needs of mind and body, and allow you time to process your feelings when they come up?

- What rituals can you do every day to rise above the stage and see the play of life with greater detachment and perspective?

- What rituals help you connect to the Spirit within and get centered in your Core Self?

When your list is complete, choose one daily ritual that you can incorporate into your life for the next week. Then watch to see the difference it makes in the quality of your life. You can add rituals or revise them as necessary until you find the right combination for you.

How do you know it's working? You know it's working when your life stops being deadly serious and you learn to lighten up and have a little fun. You know it's working when you get our of your head and into your heart, when you stop being so stressed out and on edge, when you have time to breathe, to exercise, to be present in a relaxed way for yourself and others.

Slow Down, Take the Pressure Off

We aren't going to heal if we put too much pressure on ourselves or think that we are running out of time. So let's take the pressure off and realize that we have plenty of time.

We heal as we are ready to heal and not a day sooner. We can't rush the process.

Our job is merely to show up and to do what we can today. Remember "the journey of a thousand miles begins with a single step." So take the first step now. Don't worry about the second or the third one. Come into your heart and just put one foot in front of the other.

When you go up into your head and start getting overwhelmed or anxious, take a deep breath and ask, "What can I do now?" Tell yourself, "This is what I can do now and so this is what I am going to focus on. I am not going to worry about all the things that I can't do now. I will just trust that somehow all these things will be addressed in their own good time."

Then take a deep breath and come back into your heart. If you know *The Serenity Prayer,* use if frequently. If you don't know it, learn it and start to use it in your life.

Tell yourself, "It's okay that I don't know how this is all going to turn out because I do know one thing and that's the most important thing. I know that I am doing the best that I can right now in this moment."

Use the journal space below to consider how you might ease up and be more gentle with yourself. How can you relax and let go of the pressure you are putting on yourself?

∞ Journal Notes ∞

Dissolve Pressure from Others

Occasionally pressure seems to come from others who have certain expectations of you that you cannot meet. Then you have to honor yourself and speak up. You have to tell the person with the expectations, "I'm sorry. I am trying very hard to do this, but I just can't. I can't do it the way you want it or in the timeframe that you have established."

You need to set limits and establish appropriate boundaries with people so that you can breathe fully and be yourself. People will either respect these boundaries or they won't. If they won't, you will have to take a tougher stand. If your boss insists on making unrealistic demands, you may have to give him two weeks notice. You are a human being, after all. The best that you can do is the best there is. End of story. You can't get blood out of a stone.

There are times when we all need to take a deep breath and exhale loudly. Sometimes we set impossible expectations not just for ourselves, but for our partners, for our children, or for our employees.

You don't want to become a slave driver because when you drive yourself in that way you get sick or have a heart attack. When you drive others in that way, you lose their loyalty and affection. You end up divorced, disowned by your children, abandoned by your employees.

Pressure doesn't work, whether it comes from the outside or the inside. So you need to find out where the pressure is coming from and deal with it. You need to slow things down, ease up on yourself and others. You need to pause and evaluate what's happening. You may need to revise the goal, change the strategy or the timetable.

Get centered and tune into this. Use the journal space below to identify where the pressure is coming from in your life and how you can relieve it. How can you diffuse the dynamite before the match is lit?

๑๑ Journal Notes ๑๑

68

PART 7

Nurturing and Forgiving Ourselves

Nurture Yourself

Human beings are social creatures, but all of us need at least an hour each day to be alone. The real meaning of alone is "all one." To spend time alone is to experience our wholeness. It is to know that we are enough, that we are acceptable, that we are complete just the way we are.

This is best done by sitting or walking in silence. By not speaking or engaging with others, we can begin to experience ourselves from the inside out.

Now, just in case you wondered, you can't do this practice very well with the television or the radio on. You want to avoid most external stimulation. You want to be able to breathe and be. You want to allow the focus of your attention to shift from the mind to the heart or the belly.

Rhythmic breathing can help you to get centered in this way. So whether you sit or you walk, let your breathing be easy and steady. Find a simple rhythm that you can sustain without effort. As you breathe in this way, you will sink into deeper and deeper states of consciousness.

In these states, you are profoundly relaxed. Stress and anxiety dissolve. You move from a state of thinking or doing to a state of breathing and being. You get out of your head and into your heart. You enter into communion with yourself in a deeper way than you experience in any other activity.

Your mind is awake, but it is not focused on anything else. It is just the witness or the observer.

If you are sitting, your body is relaxed and all of the cells are recharging just as they do when you sleep. Yet, at the same time, you are present and alert. If you are walking, your body is moving in a slow, natural rhythm. You are physically relaxed and mentally alert.

Rituals like yoga, Tai Chi, and various forms of meditation can help you to experience this kind of deep relaxation, calm and inner peace. However, you don't need a formal practice.

Just begin spending half an hour or an hour in silent self-communion every day. Focus on your breathing and use it to help you relax and sink into a deeper level of consciousness. Let this be a time when you appreciate and affirm yourself, breath by breath, step by step.

Use the journal space to record your experiences.

∞ Journal Notes ∞

Nurture Your Partner

Just as it is essential to spend time alone to nurture and commune with yourself, it is also essential for you and your partner to have some form of daily nurturing and communion.

Couples who live together should build into their lives at least fifteen minutes per day of sharing and listening in silence to each other. (Please see the *Affinity Process Guidelines* on my website or read my book *Living in the Heart*). Another helpful practice is to hold hands (with eyes open or closed) for fifteen minutes and allow the energy from one's heart chakra to flow through the hands into the heart chakra of the other person.

Other helpful practices are massaging each other, walking together in nature, and taking the time to make love in a relaxed, sensual manner that is fulfilling for both people. Good relationships require time, attention and loving care. Daily and weekly rituals that promote this kind of care and attention are necessary to help partners stay connected in an intimate, trusting way.

Choose one practice that you can do faithfully on a daily basis and take time to get feedback from your partner. Record your experiences in the journal space below and describe how the practices are nurturing and sustaining your relationship.

∽ Journal Notes ∽

The Power of Forgiveness

Most of our wounds and traumas require some kind of self-forgiveness, as well as the forgiveness of others, in order to be healed.

We can't be happy right now if we are always dragging around the past. We have to lay our burden down so that we can be more fully alive here and now.

Wounds are traumas that need to be acknowledged and forgiven. Both parts of the process are necessary.

If you are in denial of your wounds, you can't be happy because you will be driven by the shame/anger/fear attached to them. On the other hand, once you know the story and feel the pain of the wound, it's time for healing and forgiveness.

Many people get off track when they try to blame others for the pain they have experienced. But blaming others delays the healing process and often makes it more difficult.

Some people are able to forgive others readily, but they are unable to forgive themselves. They hold themselves hostage to mistakes they have made in the past. This too delays and complicates the healing process.

Whatever the wound, you must come to peace with it for no other reason than it happened. You cannot change what happened in the past. You must accept it. When you accept and forgive, you create the possibility that you can heal and move on.

Use the journal space below to identify the areas in your life where you need to bring forgiveness of yourself or others. The next few exercises will help you to do this in a methodical way.

∞ Journal Notes ∞

Simple Forgiveness Exercises

These exercises ask you to make a list of your unresolved forgiveness issues.

Exercise One: Forgiving Others

Please fill in the blanks in the sentences below. Write down the name of each person you are ready to forgive along with the nature of his/her trespass against you. Use as many additional sheets of paper as you need.

"I am willing to forgive _____ for _____"

"I am willing to forgive _____ for _____"

"I am willing to forgive _____ for _____"

"I am willing to forgive _____ for _____"

"I am willing to forgive _____ for _____"

"I am willing to forgive _____ for _____"

"I am willing to forgive _____ for _____"

Exercise Two: Asking Others for Forgiveness

Now write down the name of each person you have hurt and the nature of the forgiveness you are seeking. Use as many additional sheets of paper as you need.

"I ask forgiveness from _____ for _____"

"I ask forgiveness from _____ for _____"

"I ask forgiveness from _____ for _____"

"I ask forgiveness from _____ for _____"

"I ask forgiveness from _____ for _____"

"I ask forgiveness from _____ for _____"

"I ask forgiveness from _____ for _____"

The previous statements are your declaration to yourself, to others and to the world that you are ready to forgive and to be forgiven for the past. Once you have written these words, you are responsible for them, so don't write them unless you can stand by them.

From now on, you are agreeing to be open to give and receive all of this forgiveness whenever the opportunities present themselves. You may contact some of the people or you may not. But when they come into your life, whether the event is planned or spontaneous, remember these words and abide by them.

You are not to be attached to whether or not others decide to forgive you. That is their choice. You can apologize to them and ask for their forgiveness, but the choice to forgive is theirs and they must live with the choice that they make.

Your only leverage is with yourself. You can decide to forgive the people who have hurt you. If you need to express your anger and pain to them first, please do so.

And then tell them you are not going to carry any more resentment. Then detach, let them go. Set them free to live the life they choose to live. You do not have to be held hostage any more by the choices they made or continue to make.

If anger or resentment comes back, then there is more forgiveness necessary. The forgiveness process takes time and the issues often run very deep. Don't expect that it will take 5 minutes to let go of the deep psychological patterns that were constructed over a period of 20 or 30 years. Just keep forgiving more deeply as each layer comes up for healing.

Exercise Three: Forgiving Yourself

Forgiving others is just the beginning of this process. The hardest person to forgive is yourself. All forgiveness in the end comes down to this. You can forgive everyone who has hurt you and they can forgive you for your tres-passes. But if you cannot forgive yourself, you cannot heal fully. Make a list below of what you are ready and willing to forgive yourself for. Use additional sheets of paper if you need them.

"I am willing to forgive myself for _____."

"I am willing to forgive myself for _____."

"I am willing to forgive myself for _____."

"I am willing to forgive myself for _____."

"I am willing to forgive myself for _____."

"I am willing to forgive myself for _____."

"I am willing to forgive myself for _____."

"I am willing to forgive myself for _____."

Exercise Four: Working with Resistance to Forgiving Others

If you feel that a lot of resistance to forgiving others comes up, please make that resistance conscious by filling in the blanks below. Please be honest and make a list of everyone you still blame, resent, and are unwilling to forgive. Use additional sheets of paper if you need them.

"I am not ready to forgive _____ for _____."

"I am not ready to forgive _____ for _____."

"I am not ready to forgive _____ for _____."

"I am not ready to forgive _____ for _____."

"I am not ready to forgive _____ for _____."

Exercise Five: Working with Resistance to Forgiving Yourself

If you feel that a lot of resistance to forgiving yourself comes up, please make that resistance conscious by filling in the blanks below. Make a list of everything you are not willing to forgive yourself for. Use additional sheets of paper if you need them

I am not ready to forgive myself for _____."

I am not ready to forgive myself for _____."

I am not ready to forgive myself for _____."

I am not ready to forgive myself for _____."

I am not ready to forgive myself for _____."

The previous two exercises describe your homework for the future. You will get to it eventually. But you cannot start there, because you cannot forgive anyone, including yourself, until you are ready to do so.

Forgiveness work is challenging. It rarely happens quickly or neatly. It is often a lifetime process with many ups and downs and a few untidy moments.

It is not easy to forgive and often we don't want to. But sooner or later we realize that not forgiving is like leaving a huge boulder in our heart. It makes it very hard for us to breathe. Life without forgiveness is not a happy life.

So, every once in a while--maybe once or twice per month—revisit your journal and look at all the people you have not been able to forgive and all the reasons why you can't forgive yourself and ask "Am I ready to forgive any of these people? Am I ready to forgive myself?"

One of these days, the honest answer will be "Maybe." And that's the turning point.

When you are ready and willing to forgive, it gets much easier. You start to feel some genuine movement. You begin to feel lighter and brighter. You begin to have hope that change is possible.

The boulder in your heart begins to shrink and you can finally take a deep breath. Believe me, that is a milestone on the journey.

PART 8

Obstacles on the Path

Denial and Attachment

There are two primary obstacles on the path of healing. The first is the denial of our wounds. The second is the attachment to our wounds.

The first obstacle prevents us from taking the first few important steps on the path. It prevents us from feeling our pain and beginning to investigate the wound from which it arises. The second obstacle keeps us arrested in the initial phase of healing. We become attached to our pain and make our identity in the wound. This prevents us from moving out of our victimhood into healing and full empowerment.

Some of us deny our wound. Some of us glorify it. Neither strategy is helpful.

We investigate the wound so that we can understand it and heal from it. *We go through the pain, not to stay in it, but to come out the other side.* This is important.

Our journey of healing cannot progress if we do not "move through" our pain. In the end, we have to forgive and let go.

Please use the journal space below to consider these issues of denial and attachment as they relate to your life. Is there pain that you are denying? Is there a wound that you are holding onto?

The old mask was constructed to hide your pain. Have you built a new mask to memorialize your pain and win the sympathy of others?

∽ Journal Notes ∽

Addiction is a Form of Denial

Many of us do not want to feel our pain. We don't want to feel our feelings and be fully present with ourselves because that would mean meeting the pain head on.

So what do we do? We reach for something that offers immediate gratification. Maybe it's a drink, a joint, or a pill. Maybe it's an orgasm or a piece of chocolate cake.

We seek "pleasure" to escape our pain or we try to ignore our pain by burying ourselves in work twenty hours each day. We all have our unique patterns of escape/avoidance.

Is this pattern the cause of our unhappiness? Probably not. It is more a symptom of it.

The cause is our original wound. It is the hurt that made us curl up into a fetal position. To protect ourselves, we tried to seal off our heart. We built a wall around our emotional body. The wall looks different for all of us, but all addictions contribute to it. To heal, we have to take the wall down. We have to stop working or drugging ourselves to death. We have to stop our pattern of avoidance, which keeps the pain frozen and locked in place.

Getting high may keep our pain at bay for a while, but when we get addicted and our lives begin to fall apart, our pain becomes a lot worse than it was before we reached out for the pill or the bottle.

Substance abuse is a dead end and a detour. In the end, we have to come back and do what we were afraid to do before. We have to experience our pain fully.

Please use the space below to investigate how you use substances to medicate yourself so that you will not have to feel your pain. Is there an addiction—even a subtle one—that you are not dealing with?

∞ Journal Notes ∞

True Recovery

Thanks to 12 Step programs, help with addictions is within the reach of most of us.

But ending the addiction is only the first step in recovery. True recovery means not only "not using," but coming face to face with the pain behind the addiction. It was this pain that we tried to escape by using. Now that we are not using, we have to come face to face with our pain or we will not heal the cause of our addiction.

Addiction is a wall that we build between ourselves and our pain. When we recover from our addiction, we have to learn to take down that wall. If we don't, we will recover from our addiction, but we will not recover from our pain. True healing will not be possible for us.

Let us remember that addiction is only one form of denial of our pain. There are many others. We can bury ourselves in working, making money, watching television, or surfing the Internet.

Anything that takes us up into our heads and away from our hearts can be a tool of denial. We can find new addictions or compulsive activities to replace the old ones. If we don't want to feel our pain, we won't. We will leave the wall standing and keep our pain locked away behind it.

The severity of our addiction probably forced us to take our mask off. Let us not find a new one to wear. Recovery itself can be a mask that we wear to keep our pain hidden and at bay. If we want to heal fully, we have to resist the tendency to build a new mask. We have to be willing to stand there naked, vulnerable, visible, without a mask. Then we can begin to dismantle the wall and look at our pain.

If addiction is an issue in your life, please use the space below to investigate and understand what true recovery means for you.

∞ Journal Notes ∞

Pushing the River

As people in recovery know, we must take one day at a time. We cannot make the healing process go any faster than it wants to go. This requires a lot of patience with ourselves and others.

If we are too much in a hurry, we run the risk of skipping steps. And when we skip steps, parts of us remain unhealed.

That's okay. We will try to skip steps anyway and we will have to learn the hard way that being in a hurry wastes a lot of time.

All of us have tried to make the river move faster or attempted to swim against the tide, but we eventually learn that it does not work. We have to "go with the flow." Anything else just increases our frustration and exhausts our energy.

The healing process is a lot like a river. At times it meanders and even seems to loop back on itself. But at other times it moves with sound and fury, overcoming any obstacles in the way.

We have to be prepared for all possibilities. Yet we also have to show up for what is happening right now.

For those who want to heal, now is the most important time. For healing does not happen in the past. It happens in the present.

Now is the time for our healing. Now is the time for forgiveness.

Please use the journal space below to investigate your patience or lack of patience with the healing process. How have you tried to put pressure on yourself or others to heal? What was the result?

෬ Journal Notes ෬

Obstacles to Healing and Empowerment

Obstacle: We deny our pain or we have trouble accessing it.

Sometimes our pain is fairly deeply locked away. We develop a really strong adult mask with all the accompanying coping skills. We may know some of the things that wounded us as children, but we cannot access the emotions around them. We learn to intellectualize and rationalize everything. We can talk about our pain, but we cannot feel it.

Indicate below whether this is an obstacle for you and if so how you are addressing it.

Obstacle: We run away from our pain.

Some of us have no trouble accessing our pain, but the depth of it takes us aback. Our tears erupt from a deep place and often feel overwhelming. If others witness our emotional release, we may feel humiliated, embarrassed or exposed. Since our pattern is to run when we get scared, we head for the exits. We sneak out of the group, saddle up our horses and gallop away.

Indicate below whether this is an obstacle for you and if so how you are addressing it.

Obstacle: We get stuck in blame.

Sometimes we get stuck in blaming the people who hurt us. We think that by making them wrong it makes us right. We think this is the way that we will restore our innocence. But it doesn't work that way.

Blaming others does not release us from our pain. Indeed, it only intensifies our pain and becomes our justification for holding onto it. In this way, it delays our healing.

We cannot heal until we accept what happened, forgive ourselves for our part in it, and stop blaming our victimizers. Of course, forgiving them is not so much a gift to them as it is a gift to us. When we forgive them, we give ourselves permission to heal and move on.

Indicate below whether this is an obstacle for you and if so how you are addressing it.

Obstacle: We remain a victim or a victimizer.

When we refuse to bring love to our wounds we remain victims or victimizers. We beat up on ourselves or we beat up on others. Most people on the planet are in one category or the other. They either give their power and responsibility away to others or they take inappropriate power and responsibility away from others.

Victims lack the father energy and cannot stand up for themselves. Victimizers lack the mother energy and cannot nurture themselves. Typically, victims attract victimizers and victimizers attract victims. While this seems to be a deadly set-up, it is actually the crucible in which each learns what s/he has come here to learn. Victims learn to say "No" to abuse, manipulation and control and victimizers learns to say "Yes" to nurturing, acceptance and love. Indicate below whether this is an obstacle for you and if so how you are addressing it.

Obstacle: We feel special/make others special.

We compare ourselves to others and believe that our gift is not as good as, or that it is better than, that of others. Either undervaluing or overvaluing our gift makes it difficult for us to give it successfully. In the former case, we don't trust the gift or have the confidence to offer it. In the latter case, we force the gift on others even when they are not interested in receiving it.

Developing a healthy relationship to our gift requires that we accept it gratefully and give it in a natural and spontaneous way. We don't minimize or exaggerate our talents and abilities. We realize that everyone is special, but nobody is more special than anyone else.

Use the space below to journal about any tendency you have to compare your gift to that of others.

Obstacle: We are impatient and try to skip steps.

The ego takes charge of our healing process and tries to make us go faster than we can go. It puts a lot of pressure on us to succeed as quickly as possible.

As a result, we don't take the time to practice or learn new skills. We try to skip steps and fall flat on our faces. Failure is the inevitable price of bravado, carelessness and lack of preparation. When we have inflated expectations and are impatient with the process, we generally get our bubble burst.

If we want to succeed, we have to learn to walk before we run. We have to practice and acquire skill and dexterity. Then, we can move forward toward our goal.

Indicate below whether impatience is an obstacle for you and if so how you are addressing it.

Obstacle: We procrastinate.

Fear holds us back. We exaggerate the difficulty of what is being asked of us and put a great deal of pressure on ourselves. As a result, we freeze up. We procrastinate. We cannot even take the first step. We need to take little steps toward our goal so that we won't feel overwhelmed or intimidated by the task at hand.

Indicate below if procrastination is an obstacle for you and if so how you are addressing it.

Obstacle: We cling to co-dependency.

Even though we have healed, we may try to hang onto the crutches we used in the past. But, if our wound has really healed, we won't need those crutches anymore. We can throw them away and begin to walk. It may be a little difficult at first, but it will get easier with each step.

It takes courage and determination to become self-reliant when we are used to depending on others. But we need to push through the initial terror. We need to know that our lives will not fall apart even if we make a mistake or a wrong move.

Babies would never learn to walk if they couldn't deal with falling down at first. And it is no different for adults. We need to learn to do it by ourselves, even if it is difficult, even if we fail initially. If we persevere, we will survive the inevitable falls and mishaps. We will become more skillful and resilient and our confidence will grow. With trust and patience, we will gradually step into the fullness of our power and purpose.

Indicate below if co-dependency is an obstacle for you and if so how you are addressing it.

Obstacle: We try to control; we get in the way.

We forget that the Infinite Spirit is making the sound through us. We think that we are the one blowing the flute and then the sound stops. That is Spirit's way of reminding us that none of this can happen without our surrender.

Let us not be surprised if our ego comes up and we want to take control. Let us not be surprised if we become selfish and want personal recognition. These things will happen.

None of us are completely healed. There are still remnants of our unworthiness lurking within. These remnants will continue to surface so that we can heal them. Every obstacle to love must be removed if the channel is to be completely clear.

Service gives us the opportunity to go deeper into the heart of love. But it also requires something from us. We have to surrender and trust the divine to work with and through us. We have to keep getting out of the way.

Indicate below if control is an obstacle for you and if so how you are addressing it.

Obstacle: We become attached to our gifts.

The gift is entrusted to us for safe keeping, nurturing, development and ultimately expression. But it is not *our* gift per se. We are the giver of the gift, not the creator of it. The gift comes from Spirit. It merely comes through us.

We do not know how or when the opportunity to give the gift will come. Our job is simply to be ready when it does come. And we do not know how the gift will be given or received. Our job is to trust that it is happening appropriately, even when it is not meeting our expectations.

All our expectations simply get in the way of the process of giving and receiving. When we want to give in a certain way, it is hard to give. When we want to receive in a certain way, it is hard to receive.

It is impossible to give the gift and hold onto it at the same time. To give it, we must let it go.

Indicate below if attachment is an obstacle for you and if so how you are addressing it.

Obstacle: We try to feed our ego.

Our gift does not feed our ego. If we try to use it to feed our ego, it will not be easily shared with others. The gift is not given to serve us, but to serve others.

Our gift will not bring us personal credit or if it does it will come at a price. We would be smart not to be attached to name and fame, even if the gift seems to come with it.

Our gift is given not to lift us up, but to uplift others. If we try to make it be about us, instead of about them, we will turn the gift into a sword that will aggravate our wound of unworthiness.

For most of us, the lesson is a simple one. We need to stop preening ourselves and get busy trimming the branches of the tree. Hard work insures a healthy harvest. When we show up humbly and go to work along with others, the gift is effortlessly given. That is how miracles happen.

Indicate below whether this is an obstacle for you and if so how you are addressing it.

PART 9

Self Assessment and Review

Waking Up

Waking up for most of us means moving from being a victim to being a creator of our lives. It means moving from shaming ourselves and blaming others to discovering our innocence and that of others. It means moving out of the patterns of self-betrayal into a new life in which we honor ourselves and others as unique human beings worthy of love and acceptance. Looking back at where you started on your journey to real happiness, how do you feel about where you are right now? What is the next step on your journey and how will you take it?

∞ Journal Notes ∞

How We Betray Ourselves and Others

Everyone's story of self-betrayal is a little bit different, but we can map the overall territory. Here are some of the landmarks we can see.

1. **We deny our pain.** We pretend that we are not in pain, or we medicate our pain with drugs or alcohol, or cover it up through workaholism, sex addiction or some other compulsive behavior.

2. **We hide our shame/unworthiness.** We judge ourselves harshly, but we suffer in secret. We don't let others know how badly we feel. We feel like we don't fit, that we are not like others. They seem to be happy and well adjusted, while we feel that there's something wrong with us, like a screw that's loose or in the wrong place. It keeps rattling around inside, but we don't know how to find it or put it back where it belongs.

3. **We wear a mask/create a persona.** We find ways to appear normal and to trick others into believing that all is well with us. We know how to make the surface of our lives look good. We may even begin to believe our own lies and deceptions.

4. **We shame and blame others and refuse to take responsibility for our triggers.** Instead of feeling our shame/guilt, we project it onto others. We blame other people, instead of taking responsibility for our own thoughts, feelings, and actions.

5. **We betray ourselves/others.** We become a victim and give away our power. Or we become a victimizer and try to take away the power of others.

How We Heal and Step into Our Power

On the other hand, the story of healing and empowerment can be mapped as well. Here are some of its key components.

1. **We acknowledge our pain.** We acknowledge our fear and our pain first to ourselves and then to others. We find the root of our suffering. We identify our Core Wound, our Core Beliefs, and our Reactive Behavior Patterns.

2. **We uncover our shame/unworthiness.** We make friends with the Wounded Child within. We learn to love and accept all of ourselves, including the parts that scare us and make us feel uncomfortable.

3. **We take off our mask and get real.** We have the courage to be honest and authentic with ourselves and others. We accept our humanness and our imperfection. We see how we have betrayed ourselves and begin to take back our power.

4. **We take responsibility.** We pay attention to our emotional triggers and take responsibility for what we are thinking, feeling, or doing. This enables us to stop shaming and blaming. It frees us to create more mutually satisfying relationships with others where boundaries are honored and respected.

5. **We see and treat people as equals.** We no longer give our power away or attempt to control others. We step into our power and purpose and encourage others to do the same.

⚭ Journal Notes ⚭

Please use the space below to weigh in on each of the above aspects of the healing and empowerment process. Which ones are you making progress with? Which ones are still challenging for you?

1. Acknowledging my pain

2. Uncovering my shame/unworthiness

3. Taking off my mask and getting real

4. Taking responsibility

5. Seeing and treating people as equals

Postscript

Congratulations on completing this workbook. I hope the exercises challenged you to grow and transform your consciousness and brought new energy into your life. I would love to hear your insights and revelations and to have your permission to share them with others.

I also hope that you will take the next step and attend one of our workshops or retreats. My staff and I are committed to assisting you as you heal your wounds and come into the fullness of your power and purpose in this life. Our Spiritual Mastery program offers a truly amazing community where you can feel safe to do this profound healing work.

For those who master this curriculum, there are opportunities to join me in this work of love, healing and forgiveness as a certified teacher or psychotherapist, or as a spiritual mentor/coach.

For more information about professional training, workshops, retreats or books and audio products please contact:

HEARTWAYS PRESS, INC.
9 Phillips Street, Greenfield, MA. 01301
413-774-9474 or 1-888-427-8929
Email: staff@heartwayspress.com.
Website: www.paulferrini.com.

Paul Ferrini's Real Happiness Workshop

By Real Happiness we mean the ability to be true to ourselves, kind to others, and able to weather the ups and downs of life with acceptance and compassion.

This powerful workshop is designed to help us learn to love and accept ourselves radically and profoundly. Participants learn to:

- Accept, nurture and bring love to themselves.

- Be true to themselves and live honestly and authentically.

- Make and accept responsibility for their own decisions.

- Discover their talents/gifts and find their passion/ purpose.

- Cultivate an open heart and an open mind.

- Forgive and learn from their mistakes.

- Be patient with the process of healing and transformation.

- Cultivate a positive attitude toward life and see obstacles as challenges.

- Develop the capacity to hear their inner guidance and surrender to their spiritual purpose.

A genuinely happy person lives in *Right Relationship* to self and others and engages in *Right Livelihood*, expressing his or her gifts and bringing joy to self and others. These are therefore the goals of this work.

The *Real Happiness Workshop* is available in both a one-day and two-day format. For more information about how you can bring this workshop to your community call us at 1-888-427-8929 or write to us at the address above.

Explore the Other Spiritual Mastery Books

If you like this book, you may want to read the other six books in the Spiritual Mastery series. They are briefly described below.

The first book—*The Laws of Love*—contains ten essential spiritual principles that we need to master in order to heal and step into our life purpose.

The second book—*The Power of Love*—contains ten spiritual practices that help us connect with our Core Self, our Source, and the gift that we are here to give.

The third book—*The Presence of Love*—helps us understand the masculine/feminine aspects of the Divine and shows us how to embody the unconditional love that will heal us and our planet.

The fourth book—*Love is My Gospel*—looks at the life and teachings of one spiritual master (Jesus) as an example of what is possible for us.

The fifth book —*Real Happiness*—shows us how to heal our wounds at depth and awaken the joy that is our birthright.

The sixth book—*Embracing Our True Self*—describes the three stages in the process of healing and transformation and offers case histories of people who have transformed their lives in our community.

The seventh book—*The Hidden Jewel*—presents the essence of the healing and transformation process in its absolute power and simplicity.

Paul Ferrini's Course in Spiritual Mastery

Part One: The Laws of Love
A Guide to Living in Harmony
with Universal Spiritual Truth
144 pages $12.95
ISBN # 1-879159-60-0

Part Two: The Power of Love
10 Spiritual Practices that Can Transform
Your Life
168 pages $12.95
ISBN # 1-879159-61-9

Part Three: The Presence of Love
God's Answer to Humanity's Call for Help
160 pages $12.95
ISBN # 1-879159-62-7

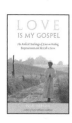

Part Four: Love is My Gospel
The Radical Teachings of Jesus on Healing,
Empowerment and the Call to Serve
128 pages $12.95
ISBN # 1-879159-67-8

Part Five: Real Happiness
A Roadmap for Healing Our Pain and
Awakening the Joy That Is Our Birthright
160 pages $12.95
ISBN # 978-1-879159-68-6

Part Six: Embracing Our True Self
A New Paradigm Approach to Healing Our
Wounds, Finding Our Gifts, and Fulfilling
Our Spiritual Purpose
192 pages $13.95
ISBN # 978-1-879159-69-3

The Hidden Jewel
Discovering the Radiant Light Within
64 pages $9.00
ISBN # 978-1-879159-70-9

Paul's In-depth Presentation of the Laws of Love on 9 CDs

THE LAWS OF LOVE

Part One (5 CDs) ISBN # 1-879159-58-9 $49.00
Part Two (4 CDs) ISBN # 1-879159-59-7 $39.00